Florence Griffith Joyner

Published in the United States of America by Cherry Lake Publishing
Ann Arbor, Michigan
www.cherrylakepublishing.com

Content Adviser: Ryan Emery Hughes, Doctoral Student, School of Education, University of Michigan
Reading Adviser: Marla Conn MS, Ed., Literacy specialist, Read-Ability, Inc.
Book Design: Jennifer Wahi
Illustrator: Jeff Bane

Photo Credits: © Los Angeles Housing Authority Photograph Collection, Southern California Library (Los Angeles, California), 5; ©Ingrid Curry/Shutterstock, 7; © Getty Images/Allsport, 9, 22; © Tony Duffy/Getty Images, 11, 19; © Durand; Giansanti; Perrin/Sygma/Corbis, 15, 21, 23; ©Tony Duffy /Allsport/Getty, 17; Cover, 8, 14, 18, Jeff Bane; Various frames throughout, Shutterstock Images

Library of Congress Cataloging-in-Publication Data

Names: Haldy, Emma E., author.
Title: Florence Griffith Joyner / Emma E. Haldy.
Description: Ann Arbor, Michigan : Cherry Lake Publishing, [2016] | Series:
   My itty bitty bio | Includes bibliographical references and index.
Identifiers: LCCN 2015045373| ISBN 9781634710190 (hardcover) | ISBN
   9781634711180 (pdf) | ISBN 9781634712170 (pbk.) | ISBN 9781634713160
   (ebook)
Subjects: LCSH: Griffith Joyner, Florence Delorez, 1960---Juvenile
   literature. | Runners (Sports)--United States--Biography--Juvenile
   literature.
Classification: LCC GV1061.15.G75 H35 2016 | DDC 796.42092--dc23
LC record available at http://lccn.loc.gov/2015045373

Printed in the United States of America
Corporate Graphics

About the author: Emma E. Haldy is a former librarian and a proud Michigander. She lives with her husband, Joe, and an ever-growing collection of books.

About the illustrator: Jeff Bane and his two business partners own a studio along the American River in Folsom, California, home of the 1849 Gold Rush. When Jeff's not sketching or illustrating for clients, he's either swimming or kayaking in the river to relax.

I was born in Los Angeles.
It was 1959.

I had ten brothers and sisters.
We lived with my mother. We did
not have much money.

Sometimes we would visit my father. He lived in the desert. I was good at chasing jackrabbits.

I began to run **track**. I ran for my school. I won medals. I was a star athlete.

What are your favorite activities?

I went to college. I kept running. I kept training.

I also loved **fashion**.
I enjoyed doing hair.
I wore long colorful nails.

I made the 1984 **Olympic** team.
I won a silver medal.

People noticed my style.
I became famous.

What is your style?

I fell in love with another athlete. His name was Al Joyner. We got married. I took a break from running.

Then I started training again. I wanted to go back to the Olympics.

I made the 1988 Olympic team.
I went to the Olympics.

I won four medals. I was the
fastest woman in the world.

Some people accused me of cheating. But I told them they were wrong.

I was sad that people thought I wasn't honest.

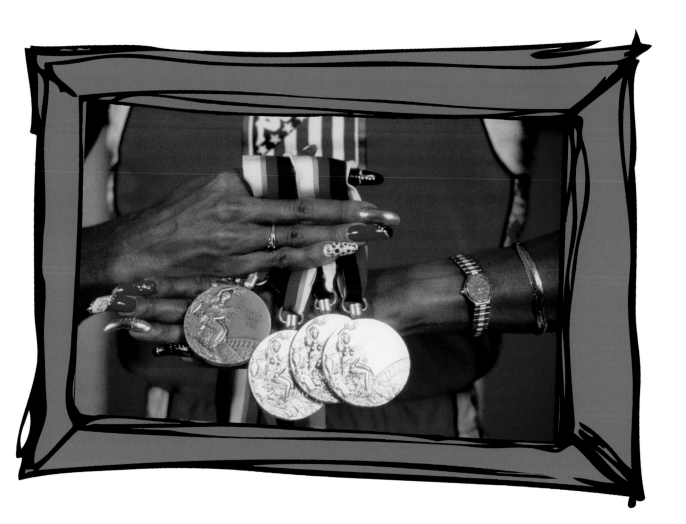

I retired from running. Al and I started a family. We had a baby girl.

I worked to help children in need. I designed clothes. I wrote books.

I lived a full life until I died suddenly. I was only 38 years old.

I was a **motivated** woman.
I ran my way to Olympic glory.
I brought style to sports.

What would you like to ask me?

1984

1930

Born
1959

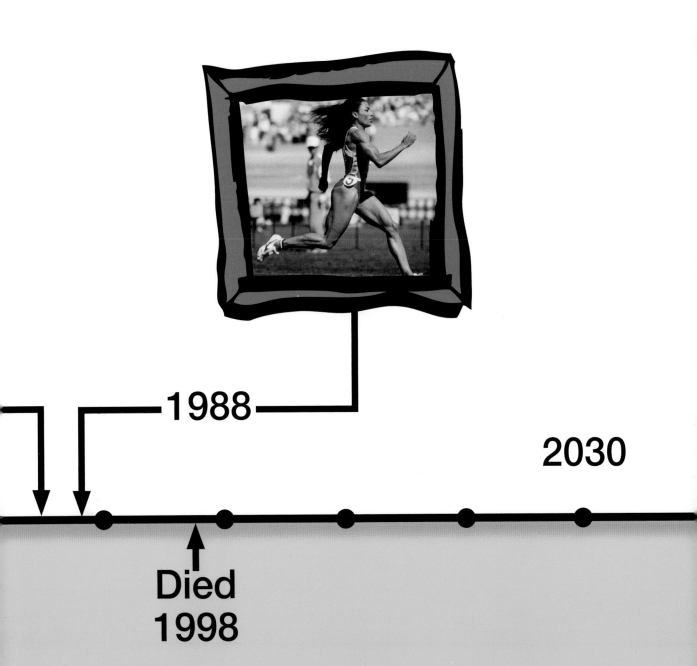

1988

2030

Died
1998

glossary

fashion (FASH-uhn) clothing that is popular at a certain time

motivated (MOH-tuh-vay-tid) having a strong desire to accomplish something

Olympic (uh-LIM-pik) related to the Olympic Games, a big competition for athletes all over the world

track (TRAK) a group of sports events that includes running

index